## FOREWORD

THIS article is based on an address by Dr. Roger Pilon to the Progress Foundation's 24th Economic Conference in Zurich, Switzerland, June 13, 2007. The conference was organized with the cooperation and co-sponsorship of the American Institute for Economic Research.

As in all Progress Foundation economic conferences, the views expressed by the participants are their own and do not necessarily represent the views of the sponsoring institutions. As with previous events, however, we believe that the analysis in the article that follows is both timely and pertinent, and will engage the reader's interest whatever his or her particular views.

### About the Author

Roger Pilon is vice president for legal affairs at the Cato Institute where he holds the B. Kenneth Simon Chair in Constitutional Studies. He is the founder and director of Cato's Center for Constitutional Studies and the publisher of the *Cato Supreme Court Review*. He is also an adjunct professor of government at Georgetown University through The Fund for American Studies.

Dr. Pilon's writings have appeared in the nation's major media and he is a frequent guest on radio and TV. He lectures and debates at universities and law schools across the country and testifies often before Congress. Prior to joining Cato he held five senior posts in the Reagan administration, including at State and Justice. He has taught philosophy and law and was a national fellow at Stanford's Hoover Institution. Dr. Pilon holds a B.A. from Columbia University, an M.A. and a Ph.D. from the University of Chicago, and a J.D. from the George Washington University School of Law. In 1989 the Bicentennial Commission presented him with the Benjamin Franklin Award for excellence in writing on the U.S. Constitution. In 2001 Columbia University's School of General Studies awarded him its Alumni Medal of Distinction.

I am delighted to speak about the constitutional protection of property rights, since it is a subject I follow quite closely. One cannot talk about the protection of property rights in the United States without first placing that subject within the larger context of American constitutionalism. Thus, after brief comments about the immediacy of the property rights issue in America today, I will focus the first part of my remarks on the American theory of constitutional legitimacy and the place of property rights within that theory. I will then show how that theory and those rights were compromised by ideas that came from the Progressive Era, which were institutionalized during the New Deal. Finally, I will say a few words about the protection of property rights in the European context, where the positive law seems far less sympathetic, yet the European Court of Human Rights seems to be moving toward better protecting such rights.

## *I. The American Theory of Constitutional Legitimacy*

Two years ago, at the end of its 2004-2005 term, the U.S. Supreme Court handed down a property rights decision, *Kelo v. City of New London, Connecticut*,[1] that animated the American public like no decision in recent memory. The Court upheld a plan by the city to take title to the modest homes of Suzette Kelo and many of her neighbors so that those titles could be transferred to a private developer to enable him to build upscale homes and commercial establishments on the land, thereby affording the city various amenities and a greater tax base. Suddenly, Americans realized that no home or small business was safe, that any time public officials believed they could bestow a benefit on the public by taking the property of some and giving it to others, even with just compensation, they could do so. Thanks to the public relations efforts of the Cato Institute and, especially, our good friends at the Institute for Justice, who had argued the case all the way to the Supreme Court, there was a public outcry across the nation over the following year.[2] To date, over 40 states have passed measures of varying quality to better protect property rights. Last November, 12 such measures were on state ballots; 9 passed, some by overwhelming majorities.[3]

But while that reaction to a Supreme Court decision has checked certain abuses of the governmental power of eminent domain, the resulting checks have not gone to the core of the problem. Far too often today governments at all levels in America run roughshod over property rights with impunity. To appreciate the nature of the problem, however, it is necessary to place it within the larger constitutional context. Unlike in Europe, with its various national constitutional arrangements and its complex overlay of international treaty arrangements amounting to the European Union, in America we have a unitary system of nominally limited national government grounded in the U.S. Constitution—the supreme law of the land—but made more complex by an intertwined federal system of 50 state constitutions. The relationships between the two levels of government within that system are hardly self-evident. Moreover, there are background moral and legal principles that must be acknowledged if a systematic account of American government is to be understood. Here, I will simply sketch such an account.

### A. The Declaration of Independence

The place to begin, however, is not with the Constitution of 1787 but with the Declaration of Independence of 1776, because it was there that America's Founders set forth the moral, political, and legal principles that 11 years later would inspire the Framers of the Constitution. And the first thing to be noticed is that we stand in the natural law tradition—more precisely, in the natural rights strain of that tradition, its roots in antiquity, its clearest manifestation in the English common law that had evolved over 500 years and in John Locke's *Second Treatise of Government*, which set forth not only the theory of rights on which American government rests but the property and social contract theories that so informed the founding generation's vision.[4] Positive law, law grounded in political will, may be necessary to establish a political regime; but because of intractable practical problems surrounding even democratic consent, positive law must be derived ultimately, if not fully, from natural law, grounded in reason, if it is to be legitimate. Indeed, so intractable are those problems that we are led to conclude that government, unlike private associations, has an ineluctable element of force about it. It is a forced association,[5] prompting us, from a moral perspective, to do as much as possible in the private sector, where it can be done in violation of the rights of no one, and as little as possible in the public sector, where forced association is inevitable.[6]

All of that and more was captured succinctly by Thomas Jefferson in the seminal phrases of the Declaration that we know so well:

> We hold these Truths to be self-evident, that all Men are created equal, that they are endowed by their Creator with certain unalienable Rights, that among these are Life,

> Liberty, and the Pursuit of Happiness—That to secure these Rights, Governments are instituted among Men, deriving their just Powers from the Consent of the Governed.[7]

Notice first that in that famous passage Jefferson follows the tradition of state-of-nature theory. He first sets forth the moral order; only then does he outline the political and legal order it entails. Thus, political and legal legitimacy are functions of moral legitimacy. And moral legitimacy is rooted in the idea of "self-evident" truths, truths of reason, grounded neither in religious belief nor in will. Thus, the Declaration's bow to theology is minimal at most: the argument stands rather in the grand tradition of moral rationalism, stemming at least from Plato's *Euthyphro*. The substantive premise—moral equality—is likewise parsimonious: we are equal only, but crucially, with reference to our rights to life, liberty, and the pursuit of happiness. And rights, with their correlative obligations, translate easily into law, unlike such moral notions as values or virtues.

The right to pursue happiness warrants special attention, because implicit in it is a distinction central to the classical liberal vision—between objective rights and subjective values. We each pursue happiness according to our own subjective values. The theory of rights speaks not to such value choices; rather, it says only that each of us has an objective right to pursue such subjective values provided only that we respect the equal rights of others to do the same. Thus, as against skepticism, which holds that there are no moral truths, or if there are we can't know them, rights theory argues for truth in the limited realm of rights. But, as against dogmatism, which holds that moral truths abound, even regarding values, and that all or most of life should be regulated by law with such "truths" in view, rights theory leaves it to individuals to chart their own courses through life. Neither skepticism, stripping us of moral foundations, nor dogmatism, stripping us of freedom, is an attractive view. By distinguishing rights and values, as the Declaration implicitly does, we find a principled path between those unattractive alternatives—morality, yet freedom too, including the freedom to be and do wrong, provided only that the rights of others are respected in the process.[8]

When it came to casuistry, the Founders understood that all of our rights could usefully be reduced to property, broadly understood—"Lives, Liberties, and Estates," as Locke put it, "which I call by the general Name, *Property*."[9] By so doing, we are better able to distinguish legitimate from illegitimate right claims: we have rights only to those things we hold free and clear—things to which we hold title, with which we are "entitled." As between common law strangers, we are entitled simply to our liberty, as defined by our property—thus to be free from takings and from trespass to person or property. But included in that freedom is the right to associate with willing associates: thus the second great font of rights, besides property, contract. Those were the two key insights of the English common law, through the development of which judges adjudicated disputes between individuals, drawing mainly not upon edict or statute but upon reason and precedent, as if in a state of nature.[10] And by enjoying and exercising those two rights, property and contract, individuals can construct the whole of what we call civil society or civilization.

But there are "inconveniences"—Locke's phrase—with life in the state of nature, most clearly regarding enforcing or securing our rights, for which the natural remedy, he argued, is government. And so it is that Jefferson turns at last to his second concern, to show how government might arise from the moral order he has just sketched. Although he does not note here, understandably, the inherent difficulty of deriving legitimate government from individual liberty, it is clear that it is limited government that he thinks alone is justified. For the only end of government mentioned is "to secure these rights;" and government's "*just* Powers" must be derived "from the consent of the Governed." Thus, government is twice limited, by its ends, and by its means.

The vision that emerges from the Declaration, then, is essentially libertarian, with each of us free to pursue happiness as we wish, to chart our own course through life, provided we respect the equal rights of others to do the same, and government instituted to secure those rights. Eleven years later, after American patriots had won our independence on the battlefield and had experimented with variations of limited democracy in the states and even more limited government under the Articles of Confederation, some of those same men who had drafted the Declaration, plus others, met again in Philadelphia to draft a new Constitution for this new nation. Wiser by virtue of their experiences with self-government, they nevertheless brought the same set of principles with them that they had brought the first time, when their independence was still to be secured. And with those principles in view, they drafted a new Constitution.

## B. The Constitution

The U.S. Constitution, like the Declaration, proceeds from state-of-nature theory: the Preamble begins, "We the People of the United States," for the purposes listed, "do ordain and establish this Constitution for the United States of America." In other words, through the Constitution their delegates draft and they ratify, the people of America establish their government and give it whatever powers it has. There is no primordial sovereignty except in the people. Government does not give or grant the people their rights through some bill or declaration of rights. Individuals already have their rights, "by nature," through the exercise of which they themselves create the government. Thus, legitimacy flows from the people, from their political act, their will; it is a function of what they have done. The Constitution is thus positive law, not natural law. But to the extent that it draws upon and reflects natural law, it is also higher law. At a deeper level, therefore, the Constitution's legitimacy is a function of whether the Framers "got it right" by granting the government only those powers they first had, as individuals, to grant it.

Here again, to determine that, we return to Locke. The principal "governmental" power we have in the state of nature is what Locke called the "Executive Power," the power to secure our rights.[11] That is the main power we yield up to the government we create in the original position, charging it to exercise the power on our behalf. And a close look at the U.S. Constitution will show that most of the powers granted to the national government pertain, more or less directly, to securing our rights, although the greater part of that power, called the general police power, was retained by the states, with only certain enumerated portions granted to the national government, particularly where state power had been found inadequate under the earlier Articles of Confederation. Thus, it is because most of the powers that are to be found in the Constitution are of that character that one does not find the kinds of redistributive powers found in many European constitutions, to say nothing of the constitutions of even more socialized systems. The memory of a war to rid themselves of overweening government was fresh in the Framers' minds. They were not about to impose overweening government on themselves.

Thus, the task before James Madison, the principal author of the Constitution, was to draft a constitution for a federal and state system that authorized government at once strong enough to secure our rights and do the few other things we wanted government to do, but not so powerful and extensive as to violate rights in the process. He did that through the checks and balances with which we are all familiar: the division of powers between the federal and state governments, with most power left with the states; the separation of powers among the three branches of the federal government, each branch defined functionally; provision for a bicameral legislature, each chamber differently constituted; provision for a unitary executive with a veto power over legislation; provision for an independent judiciary with the power to review the acts of the other two branches and, later, the states for constitutional consistency; provision for periodic elections to fill offices established by the Constitution, and so forth.

But the main restraint on overweening government took the name of the doctrine of enumerated powers, which can be stated no more simply than this: if you want to limit power, don't give it in the first place. We see that doctrine in the very first sentence of Article I: "All legislative Powers *herein granted* shall be vested in a Congress . . ." (emphasis added). By implication, not all legislative powers were "herein granted." In fact, the main such powers are found in Article I, section 8, and they are only 18 in number. And when we look at the Tenth Amendment to the Constitution, the last documentary evidence from the founding period, we find the doctrine of enumerated powers spelled out explicitly: "The powers not delegated to the United States by the Constitution, nor prohibited by it to the States, are reserved to the States respectively, or to the people." In other words, the Constitution creates a government of delegated, enumerated, and thus limited powers.

Many today with only a passing understanding of the U.S. Constitution think first of the Bill of Rights, the first ten amendments to the Constitution that protect freedom of religion, freedom of speech, due process, and so forth. But the Bill of Rights was an afterthought, added in 1791 as a condition for ensuring ratification by those states that feared the national government would otherwise have too much power. Indeed, the main restraint on the national government was to come from the doctrine of enumerated powers, as the story behind the Ninth Amendment makes clear. When a bill of rights was first proposed toward the end of the Constitutional Convention, objections were raised on two main grounds. First, such a bill was unnecessary, it was said, since the enumeration of federal powers would preclude government's infringing any of the proposed rights. And second, since we have in principle an infinite number of rights, which could hardly be included in such a bill, the failure to include those rights would be construed, by ordinary principles of legal reasoning, as implying that only the rights that were mentioned were meant to be protected. To address that objection, therefore, the Ninth Amendment was written: "The enumeration in the Constitution of certain rights shall not be construed to deny or disparage others retained by the people."

Thus, the Ninth and Tenth Amendments can be seen as recapitulating the libertarian vision that was first set forth in the Declaration of Independence: we have rights both enumerated and unenumerated; the government has only those powers that have been delegated to it, as enumerated in the Constitution or as implicit in that enumeration. In a word, most of life was meant to be lived in the private sector. Government was there to secure the rights pertaining to that sector and to do the few other things we authorized it to do. It was not authorized to engage in the wide-ranging social engineering the national government practices today.

The Constitution was not perfect, of course. Its cardinal flaw, in fact, was its oblique recognition of slavery, made necessary to ensure ratification by all thirteen states. That slavery was inconsistent with the grand principles the Founders and Framers had articulated could hardly be denied. They hoped simply that it would wither away over time. It did not. It took a civil war to end slavery, and the passage of the Civil War Amendments to end it as a matter of constitutional law. The Thirteenth Amendment did that in 1865. In 1870 the Fifteenth Amendment prohibited states from denying the franchise on the basis of race, color, or previous condition of servitude. And in 1868 the Fourteenth Amendment, for the first time, gave federal remedies against state violations of rights. Prior to that time, the Bill of Rights had been held to apply only against the federal government, only against the government that was created by the document it amended.[12] Thus, the Civil War Amendments are properly read as "completing" the Constitution by bringing into the document at last the principles and promise of the Declaration.[13]

### C. The Constitution and Property Rights

With that outline of the Constitution, as completed by the Civil War Amendments, we can turn at last to the question of how it protects property rights. It is noteworthy that nowhere in the document do we find explicit mention of a right to acquire, use, or dispose of property. Yet given the theory of the Constitution, that should not surprise. We start with a world of rights and no government; we create government and give it certain powers; by implication, where no power is given that might interfere with a right, there is a right. Thus, the failure to mention a right implies nothing about its existence. And, in fact, the Framers simply assumed the existence of such rights, defined and protected mainly by state law, because the common law, grounded in property, was the background for all they did. The Constitution made no basic change in that law. It simply authorized a stronger federal government than had been afforded by the Articles of Confederation it replaced, and for two main reasons. First, to enable the nation to better address foreign affairs—both war and commerce. And second, to enable the federal government to ensure the free flow of commerce among the states by checking state efforts, arising under the Articles of Confederation, to erect tariffs and other protectionist measures that were frustrating that commerce.

Like the state law that recognized and protected them, therefore, property rights were a fundamental part of the legal background the Framers assumed when they drafted the Constitution.[14] That explains the document's *indirect* protection of property rights, mainly through the Fifth and Fourteenth Amendments. Both contain Due Process Clauses that prohibit government from depriving a person of life, liberty, or property without due process of law. The Fifth Amendment protects against the federal government; the Fourteenth Amendment protects against the states. The Fifth Amendment also contains the Takings Clause, which is good against the federal government and has been held by the Supreme Court to be "incorporated" by the Fourteenth Amendment against the states.[15] The Takings Clause reads, "nor shall private property be taken for public use without just compensation." In addition, most state constitutions contain similar clauses. Thus, actions can be brought in state courts under either state or federal law or in federal courts under federal law.[16]

Read narrowly, the Due Process Clauses guarantee only that if government takes a person's life, liberty, or property, it must do so through regular procedures, with notice of the reason, an opportunity to challenge the reason, and so forth. Strictly speaking, of course, the clauses say nothing about the reasons that would justify depriving a person of life, liberty, or property. That has led to a heated debate in American jurisprudence between "textualists," who would allow deprivations for any reason a legislative majority wishes, within the constraints of its authority; and others advocating "substantive due process," who point to the historical understanding of "due process of law" as limiting the reasons that a judge or a legislature may invoke. The first group tends toward legal positivism and legislative supremacy, the second toward natural rights and judicial supremacy.

The Takings Clause is clearly a substantive guarantee, but it has problems of its own. To begin, like the Due Process Clauses, which are aimed simply at protecting rights, the Takings Clause has a similar aim, but it is couched within an implicit grant of power, the power of government to take private property for public use, provided the owner is paid just compensation—commonly known, of course, as the power of eminent domain. The problem, however, is that no one has such a power in the state of nature. No one has a right to condemn his neighbor's property, however worthy his purpose, even if he does give him just compensation. Where then does government, which gets its power from the people, get such a power? It is patently circular, of course, to say that eminent domain is an "inherent" power of sovereignty. The most we can say, it seems, is that in the original position we "all" consented to government's having this power; and its exercise is Pareto Superior, as economists say, meaning that at least one person is made better off by its exercise (the public, as evidenced by its willingness to pay), and no one is made worse off (the person who receives just compensation is presumed to be indifferent to its exercise).

It was not for nothing, then, that eminent domain was known in the seventeenth and eighteenth centuries as "the despotic power."[17] In the case of unwilling "sellers," after all, it amounts to a forced association. Indeed, if there is a presumption against doing things through government because government, at the initial collective level, is a forced association, then *a fortiori* there is a presumption against using eminent domain, at the individual level, because it is a forced association yet again. And that is especially so when the compensation is less than just, as happens when "market value" is the standard, as usually it is in American law.

But two more problems have plagued eminent domain in actual practice. First, in many cases courts have narrowly defined "private property" to exclude rights of use that are inherent in the very idea of property. That has led to the "regulatory takings" problem I will discuss shortly. Second, courts have also expanded the meaning of "public use" such that eminent domain is used today to transfer private property from one private party to another as long as there is arguably some "public benefit" to the transfer.

More on that shortly as well. For now, it is enough to note that, far from there being a presumption against the use of eminent domain, its use in America today is promiscuous.

### *II. Property Rights Under Modern "Constitutional Law"*

Having outlined the theory behind the United States Constitution, the structure of the document, and the place of property rights within that theory and structure, I want now to illustrate how far today we have strayed from that vision. To do that, however, it will be useful first to trace the larger constitutional history within which that process has unfolded, the better to appreciate the several forces that have weakened property rights in America over the twentieth century.[18] That larger history is one of constitutional demise and government growth. As I have argued, the Constitution, especially after it was completed by the Civil War Amendments, stood for individual liberty secured by limited government. Indeed, Madison assured his readers in *Federalist* No. 45 that the powers of the new government would be "few and defined." Federal powers today, of course, are anything but that. Because property rights especially have fallen victim to that growth in government, an account of how the growth came about will help explain the Supreme Court's more particular treatment of property rights over the period.

### A. From Limited Government to Leviathan

In actual practice, of course, the Constitution's principles never have been fully respected, even after the document was completed following the Civil War, and no example since then has been more troubling than racial policy in the South. Official "Jim Crow" segregation would last there for nearly a century, until the Supreme Court and Congress brought it to an end in the 1950s and 1960s. One of the main reasons it took so long to do that was that courts, despite their counter-majoritarian charter, were reluctant to act against the dominant political will, especially in the area of race relations. That reluctance was illustrated early on in the notorious *Slaughterhouse Cases* of 1873 when a bitterly divided Supreme Court effectively eviscerated the Privileges or Immunities Clause of the Fourteenth Amendment, barely five years after the amendment was ratified, upholding in the process a state-created New Orleans monopoly. That left the Court trying thereafter to restrain the states, where most power rested, under the amendment's less substantive Due Process Clause. For the next sixty-five years the Court would do that fairly well, especially when states intruded on economic liberty; but the record was uneven, in large part because the Court never did grasp deeply or comprehensively the theory of rights that underpins the Constitution.[19]

In time, however, the courts also found themselves swimming upstream against changing intellectual currents that were flowing toward ever-larger government. Late in the nineteenth century the Progressive Era took root in America. Drawing from German schools of "good government," from British utilitarianism as an attack on natural rights, and from home-grown democratic theory, Progressives looked to the new social sciences to solve, through government programs, the social and economic problems that had accompanied industrialization and urbanization after the Civil War. Whereas previous generations had seen government as a necessary evil, Progressives viewed it as an engine of good. It was to be better living through bigger government, with "social engineers" leading the way.[20]

Standing athwart that political activism, however, was a Constitution authorizing only limited government, and courts willing to enforce it—as courts were, for the most part. Things came to a head during the Great Depression, following the election of Franklin Roosevelt, when the activists shifted their focus from the states to the federal government. During Roosevelt's first term, as the Supreme Court was finding one New Deal program after another to be unconstitutional, there was great debate within the administration about whether to try to amend the Constitution, as had been done after the Civil War when that generation wanted fundamental change, or to pack the Court with six new members who would see things Roosevelt's way. Shortly after the landslide election of 1936, Roosevelt chose the latter course. The reaction in the country was immediate: not even Congress would go along with his Court-packing scheme. But the Court got the message. There followed the famous "switch in time that saved nine," and the Court began rewriting the Constitution without benefit of constitutional amendment.[21]

The Court did so in two main steps. First, in 1937 it eviscerated the very centerpiece of the Constitution, the doctrine of enumerated powers. It read the Commerce Clause, which was meant mainly to enable Congress to ensure free interstate commerce, as authorizing Congress, far more broadly, to regulate anything that "affected" interstate commerce, which of course is everything, at some level.[22] And it read the so-called General

Welfare Clause, which is merely a summary phrase in the Taxing Clause, as authorizing Congress to tax and spend for the "general welfare," which in practice means that Congress can spend on anything it wants.[23] The floodgates were thus now opened for federal regulatory and redistributive schemes, respectively—for the modern welfare state.

Second, because federal power, now all but plenary, and state power could still be checked by individuals claiming that federal and state programs were violating their rights, that impediment to expansive government was addressed in 1938 in the infamous *Carolene Products* case.[24] In famous footnote four of the opinion the Court distinguished two kinds of rights, in effect, fundamental and nonfundamental, and two levels of judicial review, strict and rational basis review. If a measure implicated "fundamental" rights like speech, voting, or, later, certain personal rights, courts would apply "strict scrutiny," meaning the burden would be on the government to show that the measure served a "compelling state interest" and the means it employed were "narrowly tailored" to serve that interest, which meant that in most cases the measure would be unconstitutional. By contrast, if a measure implicated "nonfundamental" rights like property, contract, or the rights exercised in "ordinary commercial relations," courts would apply the "rational basis test," meaning they would defer to the political branches and ask simply whether the legislature had some rational or conceivable basis for the measure, which in effect meant it would sail right through. With that, the die was cast: "human rights" would get special attention; property rights would fall to a second-class status.

## B. Judicial "Activism" and "Restraint"

That methodology was nowhere to be found in the Constitution, of course. It was invented from whole cloth to enable New Deal programs to pass constitutional muster. Not surprisingly, there followed a massive growth of government in America—federal, state, and local—for the Constitution now served more to facilitate than to limit power. And it was only a matter of time until those measures found their way back to the Court, the Court now being asked not to find powers nowhere granted and ignore rights plainly retained—the judicial "activism" of the New Deal Court, often mistaken, due to the Court's deference, for judicial "restraint"—but to do the interstitial lawmaking needed to save often inconsistent and incoherent legislation—itself a form of judicial activism.

In the late 1950s, however, the Warren Court—"liberal" in the modern American sense—began a third form of activism that has continued, more or less, to the present. Much of that activism has amounted to nothing more, nor less, than a properly active court, finding and protecting rights too long ignored. But modern liberals on the Court were also finding "rights" nowhere to be found even among our unenumerated rights,[25] while ignoring rights plainly enumerated, like property and contract, even as they continued to ignore the doctrine of enumerated powers.

As that patently political jurisprudence grew, it led to a conservative backlash, beginning in the late 1960s, and a call for judicial "restraint."[26] But most conservatives directed their fire only against liberal *rights* activism. Making peace with the New Deal Court's evisceration of the doctrine of enumerated *powers*, they called for judicial deference to the political branches, especially the states, and for protecting only those rights that were enumerated in the Constitution, thus ignoring the Ninth Amendment, the Privileges or Immunities Clause of the Fourteenth Amendment, and the substantive implications of the Due Process Clauses of the Fifth and Fourteenth Amendments.

In practice, however, although both camps tended toward deference to power, liberal jurists tended to protect "personal" rights, variously understood, while leaving property rights and economic liberties to the tender mercies of the political branches. Conservative jurists, by contrast, tended to protect property rights and, to a far lesser extent, economic liberties, while leaving unenumerated rights, including many personal liberties, exposed to majoritarian tyranny.

As those two camps warred, a third, classical liberal or libertarian school of thought (re)emerged in the late 1970s, to which I belong.[27] That school criticizes both liberal "activism" and conservative "restraint"—both stemming from the mistaken jurisprudence of the New Deal. Courts, it argues, should be concerned less with whether they are active or restrained than with whether they are discerning and applying the law, including the background law, correctly—recognizing only those powers that have been authorized,[28] protecting all and only those rights we have, enumerated and unenumerated alike. That, of course, is what judges are supposed to do. To do it, however, they must grasp the basic theory of the matter, the Constitution's first principles; and that is the understanding that is too rare today, steeped as we are in "constitutional law" that is far removed from our natural rights origins.

## C. The Supreme Court's Treatment of Property Rights

As that brief history should indicate, to a great extent in America today politics has trumped law. Ignoring and often disparaging the Constitution of limited government, Progressives promoted instead the virtues of expansive "democratic" government.[29] And under political pressure, the New Deal Court "constitutionalized" that agenda simply by radically rereading the Constitution. As a result, government today intrudes into virtually every aspect of life. That entails massive redistribution, either through taxation or through regulation—coercing some for the benefit of others. In a word, public policy today is far less concerned with protecting rights than with providing goods—by redistributing *property*, including liberty.

Lest there be any doubt about the modern Supreme Court's view of regulatory redistribution, here is the Court in 1985 speaking directly to the issue:

> In the course of regulating commercial and other human affairs, Congress routinely creates burdens for some that directly benefit others. For example, Congress may set minimum wages, control prices, or create causes of action that did not previously exist. Given the propriety of the governmental power to regulate, it cannot be said that the Takings Clause is violated whenever legislation requires one person to use his or her assets for the benefit of another.[30]

To outline, systematically, how modern Supreme Court decisions have undermined property rights, limiting "property" here to its ordinary signification, I will now set forth four basic scenarios involving government actions that affect property, distinguishing those actions that do not and those that do violate rights. I will then take the last of those scenarios and distinguish four versions of that, again distinguishing those actions that do not and those that do violate rights. Finally, I will raise a few procedural issues surrounding the Court's property rights jurisprudence. An outline of this kind, drawing on points made earlier, gives us a theory of the matter that is grounded in first principles, something that is often not evident in the cases.[31]

In scenario one, government acts in a way that causes property values to drop, but it violates no rights. It closes a local public school, for example, or a military base, and local property values drop accordingly; or it builds a new highway some distance from the old one, reducing the flow of trade to businesses located on the old highway. In those kinds of cases, owners often believe the government owes them compensation under the Takings Clause because its action has "taken" the value in their property. But the government has taken nothing they own free and clear—they do not own the value in their property. Absent a contractual right against the government on which they might rely, there is no property right at issue; thus, government owes them no compensation.

In scenario two, government regulates, through its basic police power, to prohibit private or public nuisances or excessive risk to others, and here too property values decline accordingly. But once again, no rights are violated. No compensation is due the owners thus restricted, even if their property values are reduced by the regulations, because they had no right to engage in those uses to begin with. Thus, the government takes nothing that belongs to them. In fact, it is protecting the property rights of others—their right to the quiet enjoyment of *their* property. We have to be careful here, of course, to ensure that the regulated activity *is* noxious or risky to others, and so is properly subject to regulation under the police power. But if it is, government owes the owners no compensation for their losses.

Scenario three is the classic regulatory taking: when regulations designed to give the public various goods take otherwise legitimate uses an owner has in his property, thereby reducing its value, with no offsetting benefit, the Takings Clause, properly understood and applied, requires just compensation for the loss.[32] Here, government regulates not to prohibit wrongful but rather rightful uses; not to prevent harms to others, as under scenario two, but to provide the public with various goods—lovely views, historic preservation, agricultural reserves, wildlife habitat—goods that are afforded by restricting the owner. Regulations prohibit the owner from using his property as he otherwise might—thus taking those uses—and the value of the property drops. If the government is authorized to provide such goods to the public, it may do so, of course. But if doing so requires restricting an owner from doing what he otherwise could do, the Takings Clause should apply and the government should pay for what it takes. Were it not so, government could simply provide the public with those goods "off budget," the costs falling entirely on the owner, the public enjoying them cost-free. It was precisely to prevent that kind of expropriation that the Takings Clause was included in the Constitution in the first place.[33]

That, unfortunately, is not how American law works today when owners bring actions against governments for the great variety of regulatory takings that happen every day. In almost all cases, in fact, owners face an uphill battle, struggling against a body of law that is largely ad hoc. Those who defend the government's not having to pay owners for regulatory takings often claim, among other things, that "the property" has not been taken. But that objection rests on a definition of "property" found nowhere else in law. Property can be divided into many estates, after all, the underlying fee being only one. Take any of the uses that convey with the title and you have taken something that belongs to the owner. In many cases, however, the regulations are so extensive that the owner is left holding an empty title. Apart from *de minimis* losses, and losses that arise when regulations restrict everyone equally in order to provide roughly equal benefits for everyone, the public should pay for the goods it acquires through restricting the rights of an owner, just like any private party would have to do. It is quite enough that the public can simply take those goods through the "despotic power" of eminent domain. That it should not pay for them besides adds insult to injury, amounting to plain theft. Yet that is happening all across America today.

It is a mistake, then, to think of regulatory takings as "mere" regulation: they are *takings*—through regulation rather than through condemnation of the whole estate. In fact, they are usually litigated, when they are, through an "inverse condemnation" action whereby the regulated owner sues either to have his property condemned outright so that he can be compensated for it, or to retain title and be compensated for the losses caused by the regulatory restrictions. Thus, condemnation and the power of eminent domain, parading as regulation, are plainly at issue in either case. Even though the government does not condemn the property outright, it condemns the uses taken by the regulation.

That brings us to scenario four, condemnation in the full sense, with government taking the whole estate. These are usually called "eminent domain" cases, but that is somewhat misleading insofar as it implies that regulatory takings do not also involve eminent domain, as just noted. In these cases, however, government is ordinarily the moving party as it seeks to take title and oust the owner from his property, offering him compensation in the process. Unlike with regulatory takings, therefore, the obligation of government to compensate the owner is not at issue—although whether the compensation is just often is an issue. Rather, the "public use" restraint comes to the fore.

The Takings Clause authorizes government to take private property, but only for a "public use" and with just compensation. Here again we see the Progressives' agenda facilitated by courts willing to expand the definition of "public use" so that government may grow. Either directly or by delegating its eminent domain power to private entities, government takes property for projects that are said to "benefit" the public. And the courts have accommodated that expansion by reading "public use" as "public benefit." Clearly, those terms are not synonymous: one restricts government, the other facilitates it, since virtually any project benefits the public at some level.

There are four basic contexts or rationales for such full condemnations. In the first context, property is taken from a private person and title is transferred to the government for a clear public use—to build a military base, a public road or school, or some other public facility. Assuming just compensation is paid, those takings are constitutionally sound because the public use restraint is clearly satisfied.

The second context is more complicated but no less justified. It involves taking property from a private person and transferring title not to the government but to another private person or entity for network industries like railroads, or telephone, gas, electric, cable, water, and sewer lines. Without the use of eminent domain, the classic "holdout" problem can easily arise in such contexts, with the owners of the last parcels needed to complete a line demanding extortionate prices. Yet even when privately owned and operated, the public use restraint is satisfied here because the subsequent use is open to the whole public on a nondiscriminatory basis and often at regulated rates. Although collusion must be guarded against in these cases, the virtue of this reading of "public use" is that it avoids many of the problems of public ownership, enabling the public to take advantage of the economic efficiencies that ordinarily accompany private ownership.

By contrast, the third and fourth rationales for using eminent domain are deeply problematic. Over the years in America, many cities, often spurred on by federal money, have engaged in "urban renewal," bulldozing whole neighborhoods and then rebuilding them, taking title from one private party and giving it to another, all in the name of "blight reduction." If there is a genuine nuisance, labeled "blight," the uses that create the blight can easily be enjoined through a state's general police power: title does not have to be transferred.

But if blight reduction stretches the denotation of "public use," the closely related fourth rationale for using eminent domain, "economic development," stretches it even further. Here again title is transferred from private parties to other private parties—often to a quasi-governmental entity, a developer, or a corporation—and "downscale" housing and commercial properties are replaced by "upscale" properties, including industries. Providing jobs, increasing the tax base, promoting tourism, and other "public benefits" are invariably claimed for such projects, although the actual benefits rarely materialize as promised. Neither here nor with blight reduction are holdouts a real problem, nor are the subsequent uses ordinarily open to the public on a nondiscriminatory basis as is true of the public utility condemnations discussed in the second context. Far from satisfying a public use standard, these economic development condemnations are naked transfers of property, usually from poorer, less politically connected populations to wealthier, better-connected people who are often looking to get the property "on the cheap" rather than at the prices the owners are willing to accept.

Finally, if this deterioration of property rights were not enough, the procedural rights needed to vindicate the substantive rights that remain have deteriorated as well. Prior to the rise of the modern regulatory state and the reduction of property rights to a second-class status, one simply exercised one's property rights, by and large. If neighbors or the government objected, an action for an injunction and/or damages might be brought; but the presumption was on the side of use, the burden on the complainant to show that the use objected to was in some way wrongful—essentially, because it violated the complainant's rights. With zoning and many other forms of land-use planning in place in most of America today, however, that presumption is reversed. Rights are exercised only "by permit," with permits often needed from several levels of government. Contrasting "human rights" and "property rights" again, we would never tolerate allowing people to speak only "by permit," but before they can make often the most trivial changes to their property they have to get government permission to do so.

That is only the beginning of the problem, however, because obtaining the permits needed before an owner can develop his property or change its use is often just the start of a procedural nightmare that can go on for years. The Supreme Court's "ripeness" test keeps cases out of federal court until all administrative remedies have been exhausted. But exhausting those remedies often means clearing vague and ever-changing administrative hurdles erected by local regulators opposed to any change. And under the Court's test, until an agency issues a final denial, it cannot be sued. Once the owner does obtain a final denial, however, if he is not exhausted financially and emotionally by then he must go to state court to seek compensation for the taking of his property, albeit under a regulatory takings regime that is anything but favorable. But if wrongly denied compensation by the state court, he will find that he is denied federal court review on the merits by the federal Full Faith and Credit Act.[34] And that is just a summary of the procedural problems owners face under American law today.

### *III. Brief Reflections on Europe*

Thus, armed with both natural and positive law aimed at protecting property rights, the U.S. Supreme Court has managed nonetheless to make a mess of things. One should imagine, therefore, that courts armed with less should do even less well. And yet, that is not entirely so when one looks at modern Europe. Although my knowledge of the state of property rights protection in Europe, whether by the European Court of Human Rights or the European Court of Justice, is quite limited, it is my impression that better protection is in fact evolving, unevenly, despite positive law that is problematic at best. Indeed, as the European Convention on Human Rights was being drafted in the early 1950s, the question whether property rights should be included at all among our "human rights" was much debated, with socialists generally opposing such inclusion, and British delegates especially concerned that so doing might frustrate various nationalization schemes. In the end, however, Article 1 of Protocol No. 1, the property clause, was signed on March 20, 1952, by 14 Member States of the Council of Europe. As of July 31, 2007, Protocol No. 1 was in force in 43 of the 46 Member States of the European Convention.[35]

That the protection of property rights by those courts is still quite uneven should hardly surprise, given the positive law with which the courts are working. In particular, Article I of Protocol No. 1 reads:

> Every natural or legal person is entitled to the peaceful enjoyment of his possessions. No one shall be deprived of his possessions except in the public interest and subject to the conditions provided for by law and by the general principles of international law.
>
> The proceeding provisions shall not, however, in any way impair the right of

> a State to enforce such laws as it deems necessary to control the use of property in accordance with the general interest or to secure the payment of taxes or other contributions or penalties.

That language has come to be described as consisting of three "rules." The first rule, protecting "the peaceful enjoyment of property," has been variously described as a general rule, a declaratory clause, or an omnibus rule. The second rule protects against the "deprivation" of property except under certain conditions. And those conditions are expanded further by the third rule, which recognizes the right of states to regulate the "use" of property "in accordance with the general interest."

Commentators have noted that although the courts have tried to decide cases under one of the three rules—and, in particular, under rules two and three, in the main, failing which they turn to the general rule—the three rules are not distinct or unconnected.[36] That seems right: drawing by analogy from the single American "rule"—"nor shall private property be taken for public use without just compensation"—the three European rules track the American rule fairly closely. Yet the differences are instructive. To begin, America's Takings Clause opens by expressly recognizing private property, much like Europe's rule one. Although it does not restrict the right by express reference to "peaceful enjoyment," as rule one does, that restriction is implicit in the American right by virtue of America's background of common law.

The second rule reflects the central point of the Takings Clause, that no one shall be "deprived" of his property—i.e., have his property "taken"—except under certain conditions. The differences in the language, however, are not insignificant. The American Takings Clause, at least in principle, imposes two restrictions on government takings: property may be taken only for a "public use;" and if that test is met, the owner must be paid just compensation. By contrast, Europe's rule two would seem to afford far less protection. Owners may be deprived of their possessions "in the public interest"—a far broader concept than "public use." And no mention is made of "just compensation." Instead, deprivations are "subject to the conditions provided for by law and by the general principles of international law." In theory, of course, that law and those principles could provide for just compensation, and they generally do; but there is no guarantee of that in the basic law of the Convention as there is in the basic law of the United States, the U.S. Constitution. In fact, it seems that during the drafting of the Convention the reason for referencing international law was to protect *domestic* investors from *foreign* nationalizations, not to protect citizens from their own governments' deprivations. It was left to the democratic process to do that—not always the surest way to protect minority rights, which property rights often are.

But if rule two is problematic for those reasons, rule three is more troublesome still. Whereas rule two pertains to "deprivations"—or the taking, presumably, of an entire holding—rule three pertains to the taking of "uses," as discussed earlier under the category of "regulatory takings." But here, unlike with the American rule, the right to use one's property is expressly constrained by "the general interest." To be sure, American law too has come to reflect that restraint in an ad hoc way; but it has done so contrary to the implicit limits the Takings Clause imposes on government. At common law, owners hold rights not simply to their "property" but to all the uses their property affords them that are consistent with the rights of others. That final qualification *could* be understood as equivalent to "the general interest." But for that, the latter would have to be a function of the former. Rights would first have to be defined, that is, in private law, according to principles of reason and the entailed political principles, not by mere positive law or will, even democratic will. Thus, "the general interest" would be the upshot or outcome of that rational process, not something independently aimed at by the political process. By contrast, when "the general interest" is defined as a function merely of public law, as in a positivist regime, rights of use cease to be independent variables. "Public policy" replaces principle. "Public good" replaces private right.

Unfortunately, the regimes of Europe today are generally the products of positive, not natural, law—nowhere more evident than in their vast social welfare schemes, which take from some and give to others. It would be surprising, therefore, if a court found that a restriction on use was not in the general interest. Thus, in the case of *Pine Valley Developments Ltd. and Others v. Ireland*[37] the European Court of Human Rights upheld a regional land use plan under rule three, even as it found that, "although the value of the land was substantially reduced, it was not rendered worthless." Yet in the seminal case of *Sporrong and Lönnroth v. Sweden*,[38] involving a proposed governmental expropriation running for several years, thus compromising the owner's use or sale of his land, the Court found for the owner, not under the third but under the first rule. It sought to determine "whether a fair balance was struck between the demands of the general interest of the community and the requirements of the protection of the individual's fundamental rights."[39] Four years later, in a similar case, the Court added, "[t]he requisite balance will not be found if the person concerned has had to bear 'an individual and excessive burden.'"[40]

Other cases too have led to what may seem surprising results, given the Protocol's language tending toward public interests and public policy. Thus, while challenges to rent controls have not been viewed favorably, in the recent case of *Matheus v. France*[41] the Court found for an owner complaining that authorities had refused to provide police assistance to aid in the court-ordered eviction of his tenant. Deciding again under the first rule, the Court said that the right of ownership "can require positive protection measures, particularly where there is a direct link between those measures an applicant could legitimately expect from the authorities and the effective enjoyment of his goods."[42] But in another recent case involving the failure of authorities to carry out a final court order to tear down an illegal wall, the Court found against the owner of the wall, holding that the complaining owners had a "possession" in their view and in their property values, which had dropped as a result of the wall.[43] Yet absent contractual arrangements to the contrary, those are doubtful "possessions."

From this limited sample and analysis, let me venture only a few tentative observations. First, viewing the First Protocol as constituted by three discrete rules lends a certain artificiality to the analysis of cases. From a consideration of first principles one wants to know whether property is at issue; if so, whether the government action takes it; if so, whether the action is justified under a fairly strict reading of the government's power to protect the rights of others; and, if not, whether the taking is for a public use and just compensation has been paid to the owner. The language of the First Protocol, especially understood as three discreet rules, does not lend itself well to that kind of analysis. Rather, second, it appears to be loose enough to allow the Court substantial latitude—sometimes getting it right, sometimes not. Third, because the language is so freighted with policy and evaluative terms, it lends itself also to judicial lawmaking—to what in America is called judicial "activism." That may not be a bad thing when judges get it right; but the rule of law entails getting it right for the right reasons and from sound authority. Fourth, from an institutional perspective, it may be that the Court is getting it right, when it does, because of the European

Community's unique institutional arrangements. Unlike the U.S. Supreme Court, which is the third branch of the federal government, the European Court of Human Rights is not a branch "of" any of the governments of Europe. That affords it a certain independence not enjoyed to the same extent by national courts—and a potential for abuse as well as good.

Finally, and doubtless of greatest importance, one cannot ignore changes in the climate of ideas. The forces of socialism that worked in the 1950s to try to frustrate the treatment of property rights as human rights are everywhere on the run today. To be sure, they are still pressing their agenda in countless ways, small and large. But no serious person today thinks that anything but democratic capitalism yields both justice and prosperity, and the foundation of that system is property, starting with the property in oneself. No Court can be immune to that shift in the climate of ideas, including the European Court of Human Rights.

### *IV. Conclusion*

Because language has its limits, a constitution that aims at striking a principled balance between powers granted and liberties retained can go only so far in achieving that end. It is crucial, therefore, that when judges interpret and apply constitutional language to cases and controversies brought before them, they do so with an eye to the larger theory behind the language and the principles the theory entails, as reflected in the document.

As I hope to have shown in this discussion of the U.S. Supreme Court's treatment of property rights, we Americans have grown ever less conversant with the principles our Constitution was meant to secure, to say nothing of the theory that stands behind those principles. The police power, in particular, has been severed from its roots in the theory of natural rights to become simply a reflection of the will of those wielding political power at any given time. The cumulative effect is a growing body of public law that in far too many cases trumps the private law of property and contract, reducing it to a subsidiary role in the American legal system.

And in this brief look at the European scene, I discern similar themes, but the situation seems more fluid because both the constitutional and legal contexts are more fluid as well. It is hard to know, therefore, just where the "constitutional" protection of property rights is headed in Europe. But in both Europe and America, one can take hope from changes over the past few decades in the climate of ideas, toward greater respect for individual liberty and limited constitutional government. Sustaining those changes, however, requires constant vigilance, as Thomas Jefferson reminded us, failing which the implications for individual liberty, responsibility, and dignity are clear.

### *Endnotes*

1 125 S. Ct. 2655 (2005).

2 Details about the Institute for Justice efforts can be found at http://www.castlecoalition.org/.

3 *See* Roger Pilon, *Stopping the Government's Property Grab*, Los Angeles Times, Oct. 30, 2006, available at http://www.cato.org/pub_display.php?pub_id=6745.

4 *See generally* Edward S. Corwin, The "Higher Law" Background of American Constitutional Law (1955); John Locke, *The Second Treatise of Government*, in Two Treatises of Government (Peter Laslett ed., revised ed. 1965).

5 As George Washington is said to have put it, "government is not reason, it is not eloquence, it is force." Attributed to George Washington. Frank J. Wilstach, A Dictionary of Similies 526 (2d ed. 1924).

6 I have discussed those points more fully in Roger Pilon, *Individual Rights, Democracy, and Constitutional Order: On the Foundations of Legitimacy*, 11 Cato J. 373 (1992).

7 U.S. Declaration of Independence para. 2 (U.S. 1776). I have discussed the points that follow more fully in Roger Pilon, *The Purpose and Limits of Government*, in Limiting Leviathan ch. 2 (Donald P. Racheter and Richard E. Wagner eds., 1999); *reprinted as* Cato's Letter No. 13, Cato Institute.

8 *See, e.g.*, H.L.A. Hart, *Are There Any Natural Rights?*, 64 Phil. Rev. 175 (1955).

9 Locke, *supra* note 4, para. 123 (original emphasis).

10 "[T]he notion that the common law embodied right reason furnished from the fourteenth century its chief claim to be regarded as higher law." Corwin, *supra* note 4, at 26.

11 Locke, *supra* note 4, para. 13.

12 Barron v. City of Baltimore, 32 U.S. 243, 250 (1833).

13 *See* Robert J. Reinstein, *Completing the Constitution: The Declaration of Independence, Bill of Rights, and Fourteenth Amendment*, 66 Temp.

L. Rev. 361 (1993).

[14] As Professor Steven J. Eagle writes, ". . . in *Gardner v. Trustees of Village of Newburgh* [2 Johns. Ch. 162 (N.Y. 1816)], probably the leading early decision, Chancellor Kent required compensation on natural principles at a time when there was no eminent domain clause in the New York Constitution. Indeed, many American decisions, mostly up to about the Civil War era, explained eminent domain principles in natural law terms." Regulatory Takings (3d ed. 2005). *See also* J.A.C. Grant, *The "Higher Law" Background of the Law of Eminent Domain*, 6 Wis. L. Rev. 67 (1931).

[15] Chicago, B. & Q. R. Co. v. City of Chicago, 166 U.S. 226 (1897).

[16] *See* my larger paper (title note, *supra*), Part V. B. 3., for difficulties with bringing suits in federal court.

[17] Vanhorne's Lessee v. Dorrance, 2 U.S. 304, 311 (1795).

[18] I have discussed these issues more fully in Roger Pilon, *Freedom, Responsibility, and the Constitution: On Recovering Our Founding Principles*, 68 Notre Dame L. Rev. 507 (1993); Roger Pilon, *On the Folly and Illegitimacy of Industrial Policy*, 5 Stan. L. & Pol'y Rev. 103 (1993).

[19] *See* Kimberly C. Shankman and Roger Pilon, *Reviving the Privileges or Immunities Clause to Redress the Balance Among States, Individuals, and the Federal Government*, 3 Tex. Rev. L. & Pol. 1 (1998).

[20] *See* Richard A. Epstein, How Progressives Rewrote the Constitution (2006).

[21] *See* William E. Leuchtenburg, The Supreme Court Reborn: The Constitutional Revolution in the Age of Roosevelt (1995).

[22] *See* Randy E. Barnett, *The Original Meaning of the Commerce Clause*, 68 U. Chi. L. Rev. 101 (2000); *Cf.* Richard A. Epstein, *The Proper Scope of the Commerce Power*, 73 *Va. L. Rev. 1387* (1987).

[23] *See Spending Clause Symposium*, 4 Chapman L. Rev. 1 (2001).

[24] United States v. Carolene Products Co., 304 U.S. 144, 153 n.4 (1938). For a devastating critique of the politics behind the *Carolene Products* case, *see* Geoffrey P. Miller, *The True Story of Carolene Products,* 1987 *Sup. Ct. Rev.* 397 (1987).

[25] The most contentious example, of course, is the Court's 1973 abortion decision, *Roe v. Wade*, 410 U.S. 113 (1973). I have discussed the case briefly in Roger Pilon, *Alito and Abortion*, Wall Street Journal, Nov. 28, 2005, at A16.

26 The most influential exposition of that view is in Robert H. Bork, The Tempting of America: The Political Seduction of the Law (1990).

27 *See, e.g.*, Bernard H. Siegan, Economic Liberties and the Constitution (1980); Roger Pilon, *On the Foundations of Justice*, 17 Intercollegiate Rev. 3 (Fall/Winter 1981).

28 Over several years the Rehnquist Court made tentative efforts toward reinvigorating the doctrine of enumerated powers: *see, e.g.*, United States v. Lopez, 514 U.S. 549 (1995); United States v. Morrison, 529 U.S. 598 (2000). But with Gonzales v. Raich, 125 S. Ct. 2195 (2005), that effort stalled. *See* Douglas W. Kmiec, Gonzales v. Raich: Wickard v. Filburn *Displaced*, 2004-2005 Cato Sup. Ct. Rev. 71.

29 In fact, as early as 1900 we could find *The Nation,* before it became an instrument of the modern left, lamenting the demise of classical liberalism. In an editorial entitled "The Eclipse of Liberalism," the magazine's editors surveyed the European scene, then wrote that in America, too, "recent events show how much ground has been lost. The Declaration of Independence no longer arouses enthusiasm; it is an embarrassing instrument which requires to be explained away. The Constitution is said to be 'outgrown.'" *The Nation,* Aug. 9, 1900, at 105.

30 Connolly v. Pension Benefit Guaranty Corp., 475 U.S. 211, 223 (1985). Contrast that with the 1936 Court's view of direct redistribution through taxation: "A tax, in the general understanding of the term, and as used in the Constitution, signifies an exaction for the support of the government. The word has never been thought to connote the expropriation of money from one group for the benefit of another." United States v. Butler, 297 U.S. 1, 61 (1936).

31 In the much larger essay that I provided the foundation (see title note, *supra*) I discuss numerous cases illustrating the points made in this summary. For a still more detailed treatment along these lines, see Richard A. Epstein, Takings: Private Property and the Power of Eminent Domain (1985).

32 For a detailed treatment of the American law of regulatory takings, see Eagle, *supra* note 14.

33 In 1960 the Court stated the principle well: "The Fifth Amendment's guarantee that private property shall not be taken for a public use without just compensation was designed to bar Government from forcing some people alone to bear public burdens which, in all fairness and justice,

should be borne by the public as a whole." Armstrong v. United States, 364 U.S. 40, 49 (1960).

[34] 28 U.S.C. § 1738 (2006) (providing that "judicial proceedings . . . shall have the same full faith and credit in every court within the United States and its Territories and Possessions as they have by law or usage in the courts of such State").

[35] For a discussion of this history, *see* Yves Haeck, *The Genesis of the Property Clause under Article 1 of the First Protocol to the European Convention on Human Rights*, in Property Rights and Human Rights 163 (H. Vandenberghe ed., 2006).

[36] *See*, *e.g.*, H. Vandenberghe, *La Privation de Propriété*, in Property and Human Rights, *supra* note 7, at 31.

[37] 29 Nov. 1991, Series A No. 222, § 56.

[38] 23 Sept. 1982, Series A.

[39] *Id.* §69.

[40] James and Others v. United Kingdom, 21 Feb. 1986, Series A No.98, § 50.

[41] No. 62740/00, 31 March 2005.

[42] *Id.* at §§ 68-69.

[43] Fotopoulou v. Greece, No. 66725/01, § 33, 18 Nov. 2004.

To buy publications or find out more about the American Institute for Economic Research please contact us at:

American Institute for Economic Research
250 Division Street, PO Box 1000
Great Barrington, Massachusetts 01230

Phone: (413) 528-1216
Fax: (413) 528-0103

aierpubs@aier.org
www.aier.org

*Call or visit our website for pricing.*